dedicated to:

....

....

....

celebrating
your birthday
SHARE, REMEMBER, CHERISH

JIM McCANN, FOUNDER

celebrati🎈ns.com

**Andrews McMeel
Publishing, LLC**
Kansas City · Sydney · London

Andrews McMeel Publishing, LLC
an Andrews McMeel Universal company
1130 Walnut Street, Kansas City, Missouri 64106.

www.andrewsmcmeel.com

12 13 14 15 16 SMA 10 9 8 7 6 5 4 3 2 1

ISBN: 978-1-4494-1487-0

Library of Congress Control Number: 2011944676

ATTENTION: SCHOOLS AND BUSINESSES

Andrews McMeel books are available at quantity discounts with bulk purchase for
educational, business, or sales promotional use. For information, e-mail the Andrews
McMeel Publishing Special Sales Department: specialsales@amuniversal.com

Project manager and editor: Heidi Tyline King

Designed by Alexis Siroc

Produced by SMALLWOOD & STEWART, INC., NEW YORK CITY

Illustration credit information on page 70.

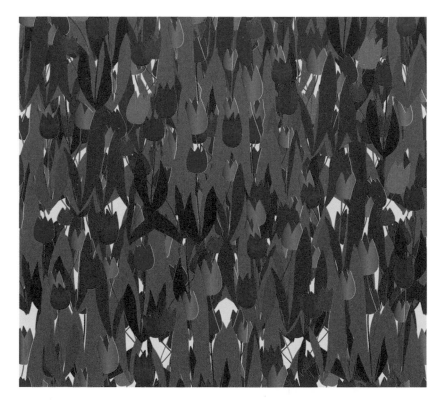

introduction

L AST YEAR, WHEN I TURNED THE BIG 6-0, my family threw me a surprise birthday party; and they really caught me. I had spent the afternoon—a sweltering Manhattan summer day— literally running from meeting to meeting, all the while trying to keep my suit from sticking to me in the suffocating heat. By the time I met my wife and a few friends for what I thought was a quiet dinner, I was hot, sticky, and exhausted. I was also completely in the dark about the real plans for the evening. When the elevator opened and a large group of family and friends yelled, "Surprise!" my shock turned to pure joy. Smiling from ear to ear, I felt special and loved beyond measure. The instant connections that I felt with all the people who had come to celebrate my special day revived and reinvigorated me like a blast of supercool air-conditioning.

That is what having a birthday—and *Celebrating Birthdays*—is about. No matter who you are, no matter what your circumstances, it's the one day when you feel unique and special—even if you would like to ignore the fact that you are advancing in years. And if you are fortunate enough to celebrate it with people you like and love, all the better.

For some people, it's all about the party. For others, it is a sentimental day for remembering the special people and times of birthdays past. For everyone, it's about connecting. Personally, I use my birthday as a time to reflect and hit the reset button on my thinking. *Am I doing the things I love, with the people I love? Am I giving back to my family? My community? My friends?* I enjoy the renewed energy that comes from knowing I have a completely new year ahead of me.

introduction

My favorite birthday tradition, however, comes from a story in this book. Every year, Deborah Wilson, one of our associates at 1-800-Flowers.com, celebrates her special day by delivering a gift anonymously to an unsuspecting recipient. It is a lesson in gratitude that she learned from her grandmother—and one that I totally embrace. After all, giving the gift of happiness to someone else is the best way to celebrate our ultimate gift—the wonder of being alive.

one oh
happy
day!

My best birthday
was when my grandchildren picked
a flower and brought it to me!
It was the first time I saw them walk . . .

—ROSELLA R.

When you arise in the morning, think of
what a precious privilege it is to be alive—

to breathe,
to think,
to enjoy,
to love.

—MARCUS AURELIUS

People who don't celebrate birthdays are missing out. Everyone needs one day to celebrate themselves.

—GAIL C.

One of my most memorable birthdays

was the time I invited my entire class to my house for a party—without telling my mother! Only when other parents began calling did she figure out what had happened. I think it ended up being one of her most memorable birthday celebrations, too! —KATHY C.

From the child you can learn three things: He is merry for no particular reason; never for a moment is he idle; when he needs something, he demands it vigorously.

—RABBI DOV BER

When I was a child, my parents would spend the night before my birthday tiptoeing around the house and decorating it with streamers, birthday banners, and balloons. The next morning, I would awake and be filled with excitement, a feeling that continued throughout the day. As I got older, the anticipation—and the fact that I could hear them shuffling about downstairs—made me too excited to sleep. It was such a small effort on their part, but it became something I really looked forward to. Now I look forward to keeping the tradition alive when I have children. —SAM C.

7

oh happy day!

He who is of a calm and happy nature will hardly feel the pressure of age.

—PLATO

May you live all the days of your life.

—JONATHAN SWIFT

Our birth is but a sleep and a forgetting;

The soul that rises with us, our life's star,

Hath had elsewhere its setting,

And cometh from afar;

Not in entire forgetfulness,

And not in utter nakedness,

But trailing clouds of glory do we come from

God, who is our home.

—WILLIAM WORDSWORTH

*There was a star danced,
And under that was I born.*

—WILLIAM SHAKESPEARE

my grandfather died the same day my brother turned 21. What should have been a day of celebration was turned into a whirlwind of sadness. We had been in the hospital all through Christmas, and to make matters worse, a blizzard hit, and we were snowed into our home. Despite the odds, I still wanted to make my brother's birthday special, so I called my friend, a bartender, and asked if he could open the bar so that we could make a quick stop. My brother and I bundled up to brave the winter storm. We ran through town, laughing as we passed our video camera back and forth. When we arrived, he gave me a big hug. That's when I knew this was a birthday we would never forget.   —JACLYN F.

birthday wish list

I WISH FOR...

☼ sunny skies

☼ meaningful friendships

☼ awareness to relish the moment

☼ a day off to spend as I choose

☼ a good meal

☼ someone to share it with

☼ a book I can't put down

☼ belly laughs

☼ blissful sleep

☼ ....

birthdays worth remembering

....

....

....

....

....

....

....

....

....

....

....

plan your perfect party

date & time:

place:

music:

snacks:

guests:

two the best present ever

This year, instead of getting presents, I threw myself a birthday party, invited my closest friends, and gave them gifts! It was the least I could do to show my appreciation for what their friendship means to me. —CLAYTON K.

Reason is God's crowning gift to man.

—SOPHOCLES

God gave us the gift of life;
it is up to us to give ourselves the
gift of living well.

—VOLTAIRE

the best present ever

MY GRANDMOTHER taught me that the best way to acknowledge gratitude for being alive was to give a gift, anonymously, to an unsuspecting recipient on my birthday. The first time I did it, I was hard-pressed to think of something that would brighten a midwesterner's day in the middle of February. Finally, I chose an elderly neighbor whose garden had become neglected after losing her husband and daughter. I set a blossoming pink azalea on her front porch, rang the doorbell, and ran to the side yard. I heard her exclaim with joy when she opened the door. Later that spring, I told my grandmother that she had replanted the azalea, and that her garden was being nurtured once again.

"That one act could have rekindled her spark for life," my grandmother said.

That sealed the deal for what has become a lifelong birthday tradition. —DEBORAH W.

My four-year-old daughter loves flowers, so this year, I asked party guests to bring a single flower with her gift. It was absolutely thrilling to see her little face light up again and again as each guest arrived and handed her a flower. —MEGAN V.

To know how to grow old is the master work of wisdom, and
one of the most difficult chapters in the great art of living.

—HENRI-FREDERIC AMIEL

*Curiosity is a gift, a capacity of pleasure
in knowing, which if you destroy, you make
yourselves cold and dull.*

—JOHN RUSKIN

One year, my favorite band scheduled a concert in my home state on my birthday. My best friend drove us to the show, only we arrived at the wrong venue—three hours away from our hometown. We ended up missing the show then taking an impromptu road trip to the Waffle House. It's still my favorite birthday memory! —MICHELE Y.

It was my first birthday away from home,
and what made it even harder to bear was that my mother
and I shared a birthday, with my father's occurring a few
days before. We had *always* celebrated together. I don't
think any present could mean more than the one waiting
for me when I returned to my dorm after class: a birthday
cake made of flowers. I still remember how happy it made
me, and today, I love sending a flower cake because I know
how happy it makes the recipient! —JAIME B.

It is always in season for old men to learn.

—AESCHYLUS

My best friends threw me a party, and each presented me with a gift. I opened the first one and was disappointed to find a little butterfly candle—not at all my taste. The next one wasn't any better: a pair of cheap candlesticks. The third gift was the worst—an ugly black vase. Still, I smiled with each present and managed to find something nice to say about each. Only after all the gifts were open did my friends burst out laughing. They had decided to see just how "gracious" I could be. Then they presented me with my "real" gift, a day at the spa. The best part to this story? I "regifted" each gift to someone who loved it! —JOVAN V.

the best present ever

Do you count your birthdays with gratitude?
—HORACE

My husband had to work on the night of my birthday, so I called a few friends to plan an evening out. No one was available, so I resolved to spend the evening alone at home. Around 5 p.m., there was a knock at the door. When I opened it, my three best friends yelled, "Surprise!"
It turns out my husband, knowing he would be unavailable, had planned an evening of fun, friends, and food weeks in advance.

—AMY W.

the best present ever

My husband—that's the best present I have ever gotten. We met the day before my eighteenth birthday and had our first date the next night! —CHRISTINA C.

Health is the greatest gift, contentment the greatest wealth, faithfulness the best relationship.

—BUDDHA

Towards the close of life,
much the same thing happens as
at the end of a *bal masqué*—
the masks are taken off."

—ARTHUR SCHOPENHAUER

Birthstones

January **garnet** February **amethyst**

March **aquamarine**

April **diamond** May **emerald**

June **pearl** July **ruby** August **peridot**

September **sapphire** October **opal**

November **topaz**

December **turquoise**

As a five-year-old, I dreamed of

getting a purple bicycle with a basket for my birthday. When August 16 finally rolled around, I ran to the front door and found a bicycle, but it was *royal blue*. My mother gently explained that she had looked through catalogs and visited department stores with no luck—there was not a purple bicycle to be found. Still, I was deflated.

Years later, just before I turned 30, I shared this story with my husband. A couple weeks afterward, when I came home after a birthday dinner, I was completely surprised to find a purple cruiser—complete with a basket on the handlebars—waiting for me on the front porch. It continues to be the most thoughtful gift he has ever given me—those 25 years were worth the wait! —HEIDI K.

When my mother was diagnosed with terminal cancer and given only weeks to live, I asked her in one of our heart-to-heart talks to contact me from the other side. A stubborn lady, she wouldn't agree, saying only that she wouldn't make a promise that she wasn't sure she could keep. "But if there is a way, I'll find it!" she smiled.

A few weeks later, I awoke early in the morning on my birthday. Stumbling around my apartment, I suddenly heard a voice: "Happy birthday, sweetheart!" It was my mother—as clear, sweet, and heartfelt as if she had been standing across the room from me. Her presence was accompanied by the feeling of pure love. It was the best gift I have ever received. —NICOLE C.

the best present ever

*My most special birthday present
continues to be a joy—my first child. I spent
that birthday in the hospital, but it was well
worth the gift of a healthy baby girl who
shared my birthday.* —KATHY C.

birthday wish list

I WISH FOR...

☼ peace

☼ happiness

☼ health

☼ contentment

☼ the ability to forgive and to accept forgiveness

☼ true love

☼ acceptance of who I am

☼ the wisdom to recognize what should stay in my life, and
  what I should let go

☼ the ability to embrace change

☼ ....

the perfect present:
A WISH LIST FROM CARS TO KARMA

....

....

....

....

....

....

....

....

....

....

three celebrating
the time of life
your life

It had taken two months to plan a surprise party for my brother-in-law's fiftieth birthday, but a few weeks before the party, he was struck by a massive coronary. There was nothing we could do: He was gone within minutes. It was a crushing blow to everyone who knew him, but instead of cancelling the party, we decided to celebrate more than his birthday by celebrating his life.

That evening, the first drink was set beside his picture. We shared stories and jokes. We laughed and cried. We ate and drank. Even though he wasn't there, it was exactly what he would have wanted, and it served as an important lesson to all of us: Never let a birthday go uncelebrated, because you never know when it may be your last. —KAREN T.

One should count each day
a separate life.

— SENECA THE YOUNGER

I was born September 13, 1983,

and, as luck would have it, my thirteenth birthday fell on Friday the 13th. Being the great jokester that he is, my father insisted that I pose in a birthday picture worthy of the circumstances. Consequently, I welcomed my awkward teenage years by standing on a broken mirror, underneath a ladder, and with an open umbrella in one hand and a black cat in the other. That equals 28 years of bad luck...thanks, Dad! — LAUREN F.

celebrating the time of your life

All the animals, except man, know that the principal business of life is to enjoy it.

—SAMUEL BUTLER

One changes from day to day... every few years one becomes a new being.

—GEORGE SAND

What a wonderful life I've had!
I only wish I'd realized it sooner.

—COLETTE

O NE
TODAY
IS
WORTH
TWO
TOMORROWS.

—BENJAMIN FRANKLIN

When I had my youngest child, I knew I would not feel like cooking dinner that first day home. Planning in advance, I got everything ready for a birthday party celebration to welcome home my new son. My friend picked up a cake at the local bakery. We ordered pizza and ate picnic style on the living room floor. To this day, my older children still remember this special party! —CHRISTINE S.

Birthday Trivia

☼ In ancient times, Egyptians celebrated the birthdays of their rulers. Romans celebrated the birthdays of various gods. Individual birthdays were not celebrated—and often were not even remembered.

☼ Blowing out candles on a birthday cake is derived from a centuries-old custom. In early days, people prayed over the flames of an open fire, believing the smoke carried their messages up t o the gods.

☼ Pinching someone on his or her birthday is an attempt to drive out evil spirits. According to folklore, if the recipient cries when pinched, he or she will cry all year. Laughing it off will ensure many happy days to come.

1234567890

Reflect that life, like every other blessing,
derives its value from its use alone.

—SAMUEL JOHNSON

Youth supplies us with colors, age with canvas.

—HENRY DAVID THOREAU

It is quite true what Philosophy says:
that Life must be understood backwards.
But that makes one forget the other
saying: that it must be lived—forwards.

—SØREN KIERKEGAARD

*One cannot have
too large a party.*

—JANE AUSTEN

THE TIME OF YOUR LIFE:

One year.
365 days.
8,760 hours.
525,600 minutes.
31,536,000 seconds.

celebrating the time of your life

The Queen Mother of Great Britain remained active both personally and professionally well past the customary age of retirement. On her seventy-ninth birthday, however, a royal spokesperson admitted that, "She has made some concessions to age . . . When the wind cuts sharply from the east and the temperature of the river is near Arctic, the Queen Mother no longer wades in up to her waist fishing for salmon."

Forty is the old age of youth;
fifty the youth of old age.

— VICTOR HUGO

birthday wish list

I WISH FOR...

☼ contagious excitement

☼ a night surrounded by the people I love

☼ melt-in-your-mouth cake

☼ blissful sleep

☼ exhilarating conversations

☼ an unforgettable meal

☼ all-night dancing

☼ shoes that won't rub blisters

☼ an evening of surprises

☼ ....

celebrating the time of your life

a time line of you:

TIMES IN MY LIFE I'D LIKE TO CELEBRATE

first day of school

riding a bicycle—without training wheels

first crush

prom night

my best friend

celebrating the time of your life

spring break

graduation day

traveling solo

first day on the job

engaged

tying the knot

oh baby!

my all-time favorite birthday gifts:

A LIST

....

....

....

....

....

....

....

....

....

....

four age
is an
attitude

When I turned thirty, my husband gave me a heart-shaped box of candy. When I opened it, I discovered that the candy was gone, but there was a clue for a scavenger hunt, with each one leading to another heart-shaped box. Finally, the last box held my present—a gorgeous amethyst ring. It was a beautiful gift, but the best gift of all was spending my life with someone who filled every day with fun and laughter. —BARBARA T.

Enjoy yourself,
it's later than you think.

—HERB MAGIDSON

Here's to my fortieth:
I'm eighteen years old with
twenty-two years of experience!

—SHELLY D.

I know it's a "birth" day, but I like to think of it as my "life" day, the one day I reflect on where I've been, who I am, and where I'm going. —LILY T.

We turn not older with years, but newer every day.

—EMILY DICKINSON

age is an attitude

At forty-nine, I was depressed about my upcoming birthday. Wondering how to shift the sadness to celebration, I received a strong intuitive jolt: I would ask **fifty friends** to invite me on **fifty escapades**. I gave out out more than a hundred invitations to friends old and new. I urged intimidated people to take me on an **adventure**, or plan something to **escape** the daily busyness. Some planned in detail and told me specifics, others only what to wear or bring.

The **greatest** gift turned out to be the valuable time I got to spend with friends in pursuit of adventure. A second, **astounding gift** came in **discovering** the amazing **creative diversity of my friends**. Traveling from the mountains of North Carolina to Seville, Spain, I boated, drove, and hiked. I tried my hand at stained glass, and had a surprise makeover in a mall.

Not all were larks—a meditation class challenged me, and once I had to fight my way out of quicksand. The range of places and activities also showed me a side of my friends that I had not seen before—as well as a side of myself that I discovered in embracing the **fun and joy of "play."** —SUSIE W.

When I woke up on that hot August morning, my mother mentioned that it was a special day. I didn't think anything about it and took off to play outside with my friends. When I came home for lunch, all of my family and some friends were sitting in the living room with presents and cake. When I asked whose birthday it was, they laughed out loud. It was mine—my seventh—and the one I remember most. —GREGG G.

Try to keep your soul young and quivering right up to old age.

—GEORGE SAND

Upon her fortieth birthday, my mother announced that she would now begin aging backward. So... when her sevenieth came around, my ten-year-old son and I planned a ten-year-old party for her, complete with jump ropes, sidewalk chalk, and a 10th birthday card. With tears streaming down her face, she laughed harder than she had in years, surprised that I remembered her words all these years. —RENEE P.

Be happy while you're living,
for you're a long time dead.

—SCOTTISH PROVERB

age is an attitude

What's Your Zodiac Sign?

 **Aries,
the Ram**
March 21–
April 19
*daring and
obstinate*

 **Cancer,
the Crab**
June 22–
July 22
*moody and
domestic*

 **Taurus,
the Bull**
April 20–
May 20
*affectionate
and stable*

 **Leo,
the Lion**
July 23–
August 22
*outgoing
and generous*

 **Gemini,
the Twins**
May 21–
June 21
*witty and
restless*

 **Virgo,
the Virgin**
August 23–
September 22
*capable
and critical*

**Libra,
the Scales**
September 23–
October 23
*fair and
indecisive*

**Capricorn,
the Goat**
December 22–
January 19
*disciplined
and ambitious*

**Scorpio,
the Scorpion**
October 24–
November 21
*powerful
and persistent*

**Aquarius,
the Water Bearer**
January 20–
February 18
*sociable and
idealistic*

**Sagittarius,
the Archer**
November 22–
December 21
*honest and
adventurous*

**Pisces,
the Fishes**
February 19–
March 20
*emotional
and creative*

age is an attitude

My thirtieth birthday was a "coming of age" for me. Rather than partying at Jersey Shore beach bars and three-floor dance clubs, I decided to spend the day at a lake house in the Poconos with my closest friends. We canoed, swam, and grilled out. My friends surprised me by decorating the house and giving me a total of thirty small but meaningful gifts. Although the celebration was less wild, it was by far the most special. —SHARMY NADKARNI

Within, I do not find wrinkles and used heart, but unspent youth.

—RALPH WALDO EMERSON

*No wise man ever wished
to be younger.*

—JONATHAN SWIFT

Whatever with the past has gone,
The best is always yet to come.

—LUCY LARCOM

age is an attitude

birthday wish list

I WISH FOR...

☼ wisdom

☼ acceptance of what has been, what is, and what will be

☼ health

☼ abiding love

☼ sharpness of mind

☼ agility

☼ laughter

☼ an unending sense of wonder

☼ spiritual contentment

☼ ....

my bucket list

....

....

....

....

....

....

....

....

....

....